ISBN 978-1-331-92546-0
PIBN 10254896

1 MONTH OF
FREE
READING

at
www.ForgottenBooks.com

By purchasing this book you are eligible for one month membership to ForgottenBooks.com, giving you unlimited access to our entire collection of over 700,000 titles via our web site and mobile apps.

To claim your free month visit:

www.forgottenbooks.com/free254896

English
Français
Deutsche
Italiano
Español
Português

www.forgottenbooks.com

Mythology Photography **Fiction**
Fishing Christianity **Art** Cooking
Essays Buddhism Freemasonry
Medicine **Biology** Music **Ancient
Egypt** Evolution Carpentry Physics
Dance Geology **Mathematics** Fitness
Shakespeare **Folklore** Yoga Marketing
Confidence Immortality Biographies
Poetry **Psychology** Witchcraft
Electronics Chemistry History **Law**
Accounting **Philosophy** Anthropology
Alchemy Drama Quantum Mechanics
Atheism Sexual Health **Ancient History**
Entrepreneurship Languages Sport
Paleontology Needlework Islam
Metaphysics Investment Archaeology
Parenting Statistics Criminology
Motivational

Three-fold Discourse betweene
three Neighbours, *Algate, Bishopsgate,* and
John Heyden the late Cobler of
Hounsditch, a professed
Brownist.

Vhereunto is added a true Relation (by way of
ittie) of a lamentable fire which happened at
Oxford two nights before *Christ-tide* last, in a
religious brothers shop, knowne by the
name of *Iohn* of *All-trades.*

LONDON,
Printed for *F. Cowles, T. Bates,* and *I. VVright.*
MDCXLII.

SALE OF THE OLD GATES OF LONDON, &c.

 SALE of three of the City gates, on the 30th of July 1760, marked, in a singular way, a dividing-point between the old and modern history of London. The English metropolis, like most large and important cities in the middle ages, was bounded by a wall and a ditch ; and in this wall were openings or gates for the passage of foot and vehicle traffic. Beginning from the east, this fortified boundary commenced with the famous Tower of London, itself a vast assemblage of gates and fortified posts. Advancing thence nearly northward, the wall extended to *Eldgate* or *Aldgate*, which defended the approach by the great highway from Essex. This was probably the oldest of all the City gates. In 1215, during the civil war between King John and the barons, the citizens aided the latter in entering London by Aldgate ; and soon afterwards, the gate, being very ruinous and dilapidated, was replaced by one strongly built of stone. This new one (a double gate with portcullis) remained till the time of Queen Elizabeth, when it was replaced by another more ornamental than warlike. This was one of the three gates finally removed in 1760. The wall extended nearly north-west from Aldgate to *Bishopsgate*, which guarded the great road from Cambridge. This gate was not among the oldest of the series, but is supposed to have been built about the reign of *Henry* II. At first there were no means of exit from the City between Aldgate and Aldersgate ; and this extra gate was opened rather to furnish additional accommodation, than for any defensive purpose. The gate was in a ruinous state from the time of Edward VI. to that of James I., when it was replaced by a new one ; and this latter was finally removed early in the last century. The wall stretched westward from Bishopsgate to *Moorgate* ; of which Stow says : "I find that Thomas Falconer, mayor about the year 1415, the third of *Henry* V., caused the wall of the city to be broken near unto Coleman Street, and there builded a postern, now called Moorgate, upon the moor-side, where was never gate before. This gate he made for ease of the citizens that way to pass upon causeys [causeways] into the fields for their recreation ; for the same field was at that time a marsh." Indeed, all the country immediately outside the city, from Bishopsgate to Aldersgate, was very fenny and marshy, giving rise to the names Moorfields and Finsbury (Fensbury). Moorgate was rebuilt in 1472, and pulled down about the middle of the last century, the stones being used to repair the piers of London Bridge. The next gate was *Cripplegate*, a postern or minor gate like Moorgate, but much more ancient ; it was many times rebuilt, and was, like the other gates, used as a prison. The name, Stow says, " so called of cripples begging there." This was one of the three gates finally pulled down in 1760. The city wall extended thence to *Ælders-gate* or *Aldersgate*, one of the oldest of the series, and also one of the largest The ancient structure, crumbling with age, was replaced by a new and very ornamental one in the time of James I. ; and this latter gave way to the street improvers early in the last century. The next gate was *Newgate*. In the Anglo-Norman times, there were only three City gates—Aldgate, Aldersgate, and Ludgate, and no person could leave the city westward at any point between the two last-named gates. To remedy this inconvenience, Newgate was built about the time of *H*enry I., the designation " new " being, of course, only comparative. After being rebuilt and repaired several times, Newgate and its prison were burned down by Lord George Gordon's mob in 1780 ; the prison was replaced by a much larger and stronger one, but the gate was not rebuilt. The City wall extended from Newgate to *Ludgate*, which was the oldest of the series except Aldgate and Aldersgate, and the one with which the greatest number of historical events was connected. After many re-buildings and repairings, Ludgate was one of the three which were pulled down in 1760.

It must not be supposed that *Dowgate, Billingsgate*, and *St. Johns Gate* were necessarily City gates ; the first and second were landing-places on the river side, the third was the gate belonging to the *H*ospital of St. John of Jerusalem. As to the *B*ars—such as *Temple Bar, Holborn Bar*, and *Smith-field Bar*—they were subsidiary or exterior barriers, bearing some such relation to "the City without the walls," as the gates bore to " the City within the walls," but smaller, and of inferior strength.

The announcement in the public journals, concerning the destruction of three of the gates on the 30th of July 1760, was simply to the effect that Mr. *B*lagden, a carpenter of Coleman Street, gave £91 for the old materials of *Cripplegate*, £148 for *Ludgate*, and £177 10s. for *Aldgate ;* undertaking to have all the rubbish removed by the end of September. Thus ended our old City gates, except *Newgate*, which the rioters put an end to *t*wenty years later.

A Threefold Discourse between three
Neighbours, *Aldgate, Bishopsgate,* and *John
Heyden* the late Cobbler of *Houndsditch,*
a professed Brownist.

Aldgate.

SISTER of Bishopsgate, what disastrous times are we fallen into, did you ever know the like ?

Bishopsgate. Sister be content, you are not yet fallen, you were but lately built by the City, *Senatus Populusque Londinensis,* in the Mayoralty of Sir *Humphrey Weld[on];* but I and my friends are like to come to ruin.

Cobbler. Truly Landlady, the matter is not great, yet I confess I have kept a Cobbler's shop under your nose these two and twenty years, yet I never saw any great hurt in you, but that you bear the profane and idolatrous name of a Bishop.

Bish. Truly Neighbour, it hath not been accounted so in times past, nor (I hope) neither is or will be in these our times.

Cob. Well, battle-headed Mistress, I heard a Sermon within these few days in Moor-fields, the best of your Bishops in the Land might throw his cap at it.

Alg. I *John*, that is the way never to see it again, among such fellows as you : but are Moorfields your walks, where you and your fellows prate to no purpose.

Cob. Yes: and verily my new white painted Mistress, and we have better teaching there, than you have at your dull *Botolphs*, or his brother by you, Mistress *Bishopsgate*.

Bish. Nay, that of my knowledge is false; ours is an honourable and a great Parish, neither is there such a famine of pious and learned Divines amongst us, like the famine of Samaria, where we (as you and your Brownists) must value an Asses head at fourscore pieces of silver (that is ten pounds English) for every piece which was a Shekel, is half a Crown of our money. How many of your Sermons have been burned, their Authors hanged, what ridiculous divisions have you of your Texts ? what blasphemous and detorted expositions, absurd applications? and amongst you the Text is no sooner read; but presently you fly from it, as wild beasts from fire, and fall a railing against rails, tell the people Surplices are smocks of the Whore (and I believe *John* you are acquainted with some of them) and

how our Bishops are like Andirons of State, standing in a Chimney but for a show ; but if an heavy
block, or sad billets are brought to the fire, there
are poor little iron Creepers or Cobirons underneath,
that must bear all the weight, and those you resem-
ble to the inferior Clergy that take all the pains :
and thus in your Tubs, like *Augustus* in his Throne,
you tax all the world. Truly now you were speaking
of Moor-fields, I am persuaded never cost was better
bestowed, I never saw them, but I have heard as
much. Why sister *Aldgate* (or *Eldgate*, if you
please) they are the most necessary, pleasant, and
the sweetest walks, that can lye by the side of any
city in Europe : they say those are goodly walks,
with four or five distinct rows of trees, which are
upon the walls of Antwerp.

Alg. There is a Dutch candle-maker dwelling
in White-Chapel hath oftentimes told me as much,
and that those walls were five and thirty strides or
paces broad.

Bish. He spake the truth, they are so indeed.

Cob. Talk no more : Moor-fields of itself is a
most profane place, they never get my good word,
and except upon the Lords day to a teaching or
exercise I never mean to come thither again.

Bish. It may be *John*, you are in debt at some
of the Ale-houses and dare not shew your head but

upon a Lords day, when their doors are shut, and all are gone to Church.

Cob. I confess my leather hath been well liquored at *Burwels* Bable, where Mr. *Geffreson* sells the excellent Ale and Cakes ; but since my conversion I say, *Go, I know you not.*

Alg. And why I pray you neighbour, are Moor-fields become so odious in your sight ?

Cob. For the great offence they give to us the godly and sober-minded ; first, they are receptacles of unclean beasts.

Bish. That's true indeed, for horses graze there.

Cob. They carry the mark of the Beast.

Alg. As how *John* ?

Cob. Do you not see how the walks are laid out, and made in the form of a cross, which is execrable, abominable, and intolerable ?

Bish. Why *John*, are not you yourself made in the form of a cross ? spread but your arms abroad and see.

Cob. Verily I am, and it is more than ever I knew before, one I see may live and learn, but I shall like myself the worse for it as long as I live.

Cob. No I profess, their four quarters are railed about in abominable manner, like a Communicn Table ; if some parishes and Churchwardens

I know had the fingering of them, I know what would quickly become of them.

Alg. You have now done, have you any more to say?

Cob. Yes verily, the Popes head is there nail'd up for a sign and makes as fair a show as Pope-*Joan* did with her great belly in Red-street.

Bish. Redcross-street you mean, but what of that?

Cob. It is a burning shame it should be tolerated, when all Papists in England are denied tolerated.

Alg. It is suffered it may be for some especial end which you know not, as perhaps many Papists and Popish Priests belonging to outlandish Ambassadors which lie there about walking to take the air, for the signs sake will rather go thither to drink a Pint or a quart of wine, then to another place, and so perhaps will you and your brethren do sometime.

Cob. You are deceived Mrs. we never go for the signs sake, but for the wines sake.

Bish. I believe you *John*, but what say you to the great Turks head hanging out a little beyond?

Cob. I say, from Turk and Pope defend us Lord.

Bish. That was a Psalm, added to the singing Psalms, long since, by one *Robert Wisedome.*

Cob. I believe it, it was long since *Robert Wisedome* was seen amongst us, he lived in the time

of *Q. Eliz.* And since I have not heard of any
or very few of that name, it was a Psalm in my
opinion that put down all the rest, beside it had
been an excellent tune, my father when he lived in
Goose-toft, would often whistle it at plough.

Alg. But what say you *John* to the trees, so
evenly planted and thriving, which with their eye-
pleasing green and cool shadow in the hot Summer
give so great delight and content to the whole City.

Cob. They look (me thinks) like so many of
your Bishops Standing about the Communion rails
to defend them.

Alg. Against such as you are it may be.

Cob. Nay they look like Bishops for all the
world for there are Some poor underling trees
besides them which cannot thrive and Prosper,
because those greater over-drop them, keep the sun
from them, or suck from the earth the Juice which
should nourish them, to themselves.

Bish. But what is the reason they are called
Moorfields, can you tell me *John* with all the wit
you have ?

Cobler. Because it may be there are more fields
in England beside these.

Alg. That is without doubt.

Cob. Or rather because more learned and godly
teaching by us and our brethren is here exercised
than in the City or the whole land beside, or it may

be they are so called from a Blackamoor set over an Alley gate in these fields.

Bish. Nay *John* now you have overshot yourself.

Cob. I talk of Moorfields and not of Finsbury : there indeed is shooting and no preaching.

Bish. But neighbour *John Cobbler* let me tell you in good earnest, when I was built new in the time of K. *Richard* the second, (whose statue in stone holding his unfortune and broken Sceptre in his hand, I bear upon my Frontispiece, on the other side *Wenceslaus* his wives father the Emperor, yet many say it was K. *Edward* the 3.) certain calves tied about the necks with withs[1] being brought for a present to *Wat Tyler* and his Rebels then in Smithfield, whom, (let me tell you by the way) K. *Richard* could plainly discern from Long Acre, so rare were houses and buildings in the Suburbs in those days) were all stifled and drowned in those fields, which were nothing else but a Moor or Quagmire whence they took their name, nay it was such within these 40. or 50. years. Sister Algate had they brought by your way, (the common road of calves) they had been out of danger.

Cob. Verily Mrs. Aldgate I have known of late years many calves to have been brought out of Essex and other places unto your Gate, where when they should have entered, their simple country drivers

---

[1]WITHS.—Twigs of willow ; *t*wisted flexible rod*s*.

would not suffer them, but drave them home again.

Alg. They were simple indeed, but what **was** their meaning so to do?

Cob. Why, I will tell you, you carry upon your top **two** huge Giants in Armour, holding up and ready as it were to throw down mighty bullets, who affright both the calves and the Countrymen, that I have heard some protest that for their lives they could not persuade the driver to venture them through, this was at their first setting up, and I well remember in that year Veal wes so scarce at Leaden Hall, that hardly any could be got for money.

Bish. *John* they were placed there to shew the ancient defence of Ports, which when the enemy offered to assail or break open, Armed men stood aloft and threw down huge stones, piece of timber and such like, to kill or knock them down, **but I** hear *John* Cobbler you are a pretender to Divinity, and are ready to turn Preacher.

Cob. Why not I as well as *Walker* the Iron-monger.[1]

Alg. I think you never come to any of our Churches io the City.

Cob. Very seldom; yes, I was half a year since at *Annes* within Aldersgate, and once a fortnight ago at *Margets* in Westminster.

[1]WALKER, THE IRONMONGER.—See John Taylor's Tract on this person.

Bish. St. *Margarets* you should say.

Cob. The matter is not great, they were built by the Papists and smell of superstition to this day, for name any Church about the City that was built in time of the Gospel, Cree-church[1] excepted, and that by Tuttle-street[2] in Westminster not yet execrated, as they call it.

Alg. Consecrated thou wouldst say, that indeed is new, but Cree-Church was new built upon an old foundation, if we should be all of your opinion : we should come to no Church at all, but hear Sermons in woods as you do.

Cob. Did not *John* Baptist preach in the desert or wilderness? And multitudes of people followed to hear him.

Bish. *John* you are much deceived, that was no obscure place like *St. Johns* wood whether you and your fellows go, but a woody Country wherein were many Towns and Cities, like the forest of Sherwood in Nottinghamshire inhabited with many people.

Cob. I will never believe that, for all I am a Translator[3] myself.

[1]CREE CHURCH.—St. Catherine Cree or Christ Church, a church on the north side of Leadenhall-street, and in Aldgate Ward. The church described by Stow was taken down 1628, and the present building consecrated by Laud (when Bishop of London) on the 16th January, 1630-1.—"August 18th, 1667. To Cree Church, to see it how it is, but I find no alteration there, as they say there was, for my Lord Mayor and Aldermen to come to sermon, as they do every Sunday, as they did formerly to Pauls."—*Pepys'* Diary.

[2]TUTTLE-STREET.—*i.e.*, Tothill-*street*.

[3]TRANSLATOR, a cobbler.

Alg. But *John* I pray thee tell me how **camest** thou to be a Brownist[1] at the first.

Bish. I have heard that the first beginner of Sect was a miserable Doctor in the University who sold his commons and seized away his part of white-bread and liv'd all the week with a sixpenny brown loaf, which occasion gave you all your names.

Cob. No our first father was Mr. *Browne* parson of a church in Northamptonshire where he died after his many persecutions among the wicked.

Alg. So he that would have no Church was afterwards parson of a Church.

Bish. But I assure you *John* he recanted his opinions, and died an Orthodox Protestant and an honest man, it is true he was persecuted in all places, he fled into Scotland, and had been hanged, had he not been near a kin unto the L. Treasurer *Cecil*, (for he was a Gentleman born, and of an ancient family of the *Brownes* of Tolthorpe) besides he was endued with many good and gentle qualities, among the rest he was a singular good Lutenist, and he made his Son *Timothy* usually on Sundays bring his Viol to Church and play the Bass to the Psalms that were sung, so far as he (like you and your fellows) from being an enemy to Church Music.

[1] BROWNISTS.—A name given to the disciples of Robert Brown, a celebrated Nonconformist and schoolmaster in Southwark about 1580; they were in those days the constant objects of popular satire and persecution. Brown, after 32 imprisonments, eventually conformed to the Established Church.

"I had as lief be a *Brownist* as a politician."
Shakespeare's Twelfth Night, Act iii., sc. 2.

Cob. I would have given all the Shoes in my shop I had known so much before. But Landlady Bishopsgate, and Mrs. Aldgate, time calls me away, I have three pair of boots to mend for the Norwich foot-post, and a pair of shoes for honest Mr. *Sacchar* of Botolphs, and I hope ere long we shall meet, and then 'yfaith I will have a fling at you and your name-sake the Bishops.

Bish. Well *John* I shall defend those Bishops well enough, and will Petition that those Reverend men may have their liberty to go abroad in the days, and repair to their Brother in the Tower again at night, Farewell.

Zeal over-heated:

A Relation of a lamentable fire which happened at *Oxford* two nights before *Christ-tide*, in a religious Brothers shop, who though he laboured in all men's trades, yet his trades were fewer than his tricks, to fetch over the wicked, that he might afford the godly a better Penny-worth.

To the Tune of *Chivey Chace.*

A Ttend you brethren, every one,
  And listen with a pair
Of swaggering ears, which have outgrown
  By many an inch the hair :
Of Popish flames I will relate
  to you a doleful story,
Which turned a zealous shop of late
  into a Purgatory.

There dwells in Oxon near the place
  where holy Chornish teacheth,
One that in all trades hath such grace,
  the wicked he o'er-reaches.
This brother first a Stoick was
  Peripateticall ;
For 'bout the world as he did pass,
  his wealth he carried all.

But when his sins had made his pack
  Too heavy for his shoulder,
I' th' foresaid place he eased his back,
  and turned a staid householder.
In all occasions by and by
  He grew so great a Meddler,
That if th' Exchange his shop stood nigh,
  you'd take him for no Pedlar.

By slight of tongue he could fetch o'er
  all Sparks that came unto him,
Except those which two nights before
  Christ-tide had like to undo him.
When he to sleep himself had set,
  and dreamed of no more fire,
Than those his zeal and little Pet
  kindled in his desire.

He heard some cry, Fire, fire, amain,
  and said that were he slack,
Great John of All trades would again
  be brought to his first pack:
Then hasting down to see what burned,
  the smoke did almost stop
His breath: the new Exchange was turned
  to a Tobacco shop.

His wife came down at that report,
  her clothes hung in such pickle,
As she were new come from the sport
  after a Conventicle:
And first in these flames she espied
  a pure Geneva Bible,
With gilded leaves, and strings beside,
  that were not contemptible.

The Second Part to the Same Tune.

BUT with less grief he could have seen't
  as he then said to some one,
Had but the Apocrypha been in't,
  and Prayers that we call Common:
The Practice there of Piety,
  and good St. Katherine Stubs
Were martyr'd, which oft quoted he
  had heard in several Tubs.

Then being of his Dods bereft,
  and Cleavers all and some,
You may presume that there was left
  of comforts never a Crum.
A chest of Cambricks and Holland
  was turned to a box of t'nde',
His virgins topers out were brand,
  th' Extinguishers could not hinder.

They that his Taffities did see,
  and various Ribbonds straight
Concluded that in burnt silks he
  was richly worth his weight:
His Hobby-horses erst so tame,
  some babes of grace might run
A race upon them, now became
  but as the Steeds o' th' Sun.

Of Canes there smoaking lay great store,
  his eyes had soon espi'd them,
They never were fire canes before,
  though he had oft beli'd them.
Mirrors and Prospectives then might
  be burning glasses call'd:
The fever grew so hot that night,
  the periwigs grew bald.

The Mouse-traps, Fly-traps, and whole
   shelves
  of whips, with other some
Such dreadful instruments themselves
  suffer'd a martyrdom:
But to conclude, the flame being done,
  some that were there did swear,
Though Christ-tide were not yet begun,
  Yet was Ash-Wednesday there.

Dear brethren, be not then too hot,
  for if unto your harm
Your zeal like this take fire, I what,
  you'll wish 'twere but luke-warm.
God bless the King, the Queen and Issue,
  Nobles and Parliament
And may all such affrightments miss you
  of the furious element.

And keep all from disasters,
And such as now good servants are,
May never prove bad masters.

FINIS.

UTL AT DOWNSVIEW

D RANGE BAY SHLF POS ITEM C
39 14 06 09 04 020 8